JUST
TRYING
TO HELP

Awesome Date Night Tips!

JUST TRYING TO HELP

Supercharge Your Relationship With Mind-Blowing Date Night Ideas

MALIK BRICE

Just Trying to Help
Supercharge Your Relationship with Mind-Blowing Date Night Ideas

Soft cover ISBN: 978-1-7355280-7-6

For Worldwide Distribution.

Printed in U.S.A.

DEDICATION

This book is dedicated to my late father, Michael F. Brice. My main man passed away on July 3, 2018 after a yearlong battle with Pancreatic Cancer. He fought it for a while until the big man upstairs told him it was time to rest. He was the epitome of a man and a father. I owe a lot to him. He will forever be remembered and never forgotten. He taught us many things just by leading by example. It's hard for us sometimes but I know he would want us to continue to live and he will live through us.

I can't leave my mother, Sylvia Brice, out of the equation. She is the strong one in the family and sometimes I wonder how she can keep it together. But then I think about the faith she has in God and how much she believes in His will. I think no matter how old I get she will always mother me. That's just how she is, always giving and willing to help.

ACKNOWLEDGMENTS

I would like to thank my twin brother, Mike B., who has always been supportive and encouraging through everything. When I started posting my tips on Facebook, he was one of the people I thought about. I would think to myself, I have to make sure the tip is something I or my brother would do. I would also like to acknowledge Alicia who told me on several occasions that I need to put my tips in a book. Initially, I brushed off the idea but then it became something I wanted to do.

I would like to thank my boy Nate Noriega, who would give me ideas for a book title. I have to acknowledge Synetheia for inviting me to write a blog for her website and participate in her Facebook Live with Dear Single Sister. This opportunity restarted the writing process. I would like to thank my best friend Morgan who always had my back no matter what the situation is. I certainly have to thank QuaShuanna who's been supportive, encouraging, and pushing me to do better, be better, and move outside of my comfort zone. Finally, to my Facebook friends who read all of my tips, commented, thanked me, and actually put them to use: You guys rock!

CONTENTS

INTRODUCTION

It is common that as the loving relationship advances, busy lovers begin to take one another for granted. Typically, the initial thing that falls off in a long-standing romantic relationship is the high-quality time spent with each other developing the relationship. Putting together a date night is a fantastic way for couples to stay connected regardless of how busy their schedules are.

What Exactly is Date Night?

Date night is usually a way to rekindle or recall on the times when you both began dating, along with the giddiness it made you feel. For many, while in the dating period, both people are on their finest behaviors and arguments and quarrels are kept to a minimum. Some people believe that once they 'got' the person they desire, they are no longer courting. This commonly tends to make one or both complacent. Complacency is the silent destroyer of relationships. Date night is a way of changing the ho-hum and converting it into ooh... hun!

You should have a date night set aside every week, or if you maintain an extremely busy schedule or are not local to the other, every two weeks. Do things that make your partner look forward to the evening as a little getaway or simply a night of pleasure that is different from the routine. Let your date nights be spontaneous and fun, leading anywhere, not routine in any way. Whether you're at home, at the movies, or at a restaurant, make sure you're BOTH enjoying the experience, and use that time to talk to each other, a lot, about everything, but try not to focus on negative aspects as that may kill the mood. Maximize the date night to get closer to each other and strengthen your bond.

Before I start rolling out date night ideas for you to choose from, here are five ways couples can capitalize on their date nights to improve their emotional connection.

1. Recapture the excitement of hanging out together with no actual agenda or activity.

Date nights will open your eyes to see and tap into more vital traits and parts of the person you fell in love with and you get to recharge the batteries of your connection. For both of you, authentic, genuine, and unstressed aspects and characteristics of yourself get to be revealed. A date night helps you experience each other's essence in a free and fun environment.

2. You both get a chance to dress up and feel attractive and desirable.

Living with your partner might make it hard to continually feel physically and emotionally attractive especially when you have to deal with chores and daily life and work demands. Conflict and tension will not inspire you to keep yourself fit and looking gorgeous all the time. Not feeling close emotionally will disrupt the incentive to make yourself physically desirable. Date night solves this problem as it gives you a regular weekly opportunity to press the reset button and refresh the attraction process. Making the effort to look great always for both of you boosts the value of the investment you are making in the time you spend with each other.

When you dress up, you'll feel sexy and attractive and you can then approach your partner in a unique way that only you can. Instead of seeing someone who arrived late or forgot to pick up your dry cleaning or did something else wrong, you can see, smell, and touch someone who excites you and makes you feel alive and wanted.

3. Committing to a specific time together increases confidence that you are valued and important to each other.
Being chosen as 'the only one' your partner wants to spend time with is indeed a special feeling. It sometimes gets lost when your routine takes over your day and your relationship needs get put off or put on hold. Feeling

sought after is a huge turn on for both sides, sexually and also emotionally. Both of you can feel confident and have a good sense of self in the time you're spending with each other. Feeling good about yourself will make you a solid person that is more relatable and fun to be with.

4. Share your deepest dreams, fears, and hopes.

An important aspect of intimacy is feeling safe and free enough to share dreams about your life with each other. It lets your partner see your inner self. This will build trust, create empathy, and mutual comforting especially when sharing things that may not be too pretty. The delicate nature of exposing your deepest dreams, fears, and hopes with your partner and being accepted is the vital core of emotional intimacy.

5. Provides an atmosphere of togetherness where you both have the opportunity to work on entrenched and thorny family issues, lifestyle, and other issues together.

Struggling with daily life can sometimes make it hard to find room to listen to each other's point of view when you just want the problem solved. A date night gives you the incentive to check in with and check up on each other, evaluate where you are coming from, and solve the issues together, rather than criticize each other for dropping the ball.

Starting the Date Night?

When preparing a date night, it is advisable to pick a day of the week that is perfect for both parties, when there will be fewer possibilities for having to reschedule. It is good to likewise consider the proposed start and perhaps the end of date night. For some people, just a few hours are fine; for others, date night implies all through the night. Decide what the perfect day and time that both people can easily, actively, and freely participate in date night. When you finally settle on a day and time for the date, it is also good to establish the ground rules and expectations. These rules will include reasons why as well as under what circumstances a date night may be broken, and what the penalties for breaking the date night should be; don't be too strict with these. Try something fun here as well. You could also choose an alternative night should unavoidable circumstances arise.

Planning the Date Night

It takes two committed people working on the relationship to make and preserve the relationship. Being an established couple, both parties need to make an effort to participate in planning the date night. It could be best if each person alternates every other week in planning the date night for the other person. Choose fun-based activities that both parties love doing and actively can join. Thinking outside the box and trying to be different every time, you can take your pick from a wide range of date night tips we have for you. Don't be satisfied with routine whenever it's your turn to arrange date night. Don't hesitate to try something totally new or pick something that you both are interested in trying out but have never done.

When you want to plan a date night for talking, make sure you keep the chat positive and be reflective on your feelings and thoughts, the excellent times you guys have, and great times yet to come. Date night is not the time nor the place to air grievances or dump on the other person. Keep in mind that the reason that you want to plan and maintain a date night is mainly that you want to continue to build on the intimacy that has already been attained.

Maintaining the Date Night
The key reason to starting and planning a date night is ensuring that you keep the date night going. You must make your best effort best

to ensure sure that nothing stops or prevents you from enjoying numerous date nights all throughout your relationship. Unavoidably, because of time, circumstances, or work, date night could be missed or suspended. One of the better tips on how to keep a date night is to create SPP's (Sexual Penalty Points) for the person that skips a date night. This really is a pleasurable and harmless way that both people win, whenever a date night is missed. Sit together to make a list of postcards with various sensual acts that someone can choose from when an SPP has been assessed.

Yet another excellent way to keep date night is simply to give friendly reminders as well as hints about what could possibly be expected in the next date night. Often, the tease or contemplation of what could be expected on date night is sufficient to intrigue the other party to ensure they don't miss it. Obviously, you should be prepared to match the expectation! Delivering hints and leaving reminder notes as to what you have planned for date night is an excellent way to keep both parties interested in wanting to keep the date night alive.

Before we delve right into the different categories of date night tips, let me provide a few tips to get your creative juices flowing:

Tip #1: Dinner
This is a fairly obvious date night idea, right? To spice it up, how about choosing a new restaurant each time.

Tip #2: Gallery or exhibition
Depending on their opening hours, some galleries and exhibitions have 'late nights' to allow people who are working during the day to come along after work. If you're both into art, you could take a stroll through the national gallery and let the art do the intriguing.

Tip #3: Picnic in the park
You could organize a picnic basket with a blanket and your partner's favorite food and choose a location with a great view for the sunset or view over the city, beach, or any other special place both of you like. Feel free to try out a place you've never been to before.

Tip #4: Explore your town
You can drive to a part of town you don't usually go to. Either you might have something already planned or you plan to explore new, interesting places.

Tip #5: Drinks somewhere special
You have your favorite place to go for a drink after work. Find a special bar that might have

views over your city or just recently opened. Order a surprise drink or try out new mixes with your partner.

Tip #6: Movie night extraordinaire
Many cities nowadays have an outdoor cinema in the summer months or special event cinemas, or you could go to the regular cinema if those aren't available. Pick a movie you are both interested in; don't be selfish.

Tip #7: Candlelight dinner at home
Cook your partner's favorite dish and make it a special event with candles and music—whatever you can think of that would make your partner say, "Wow!" You can ask him or her to go out for a while or maybe even trick him or her into going out during your preparations so it will be a surprise.

Tip #8: Create a relaxation evening
Discover your partner's preferred way of relaxing: is it having a bath or getting a massage? Or does her or she like to cuddle on the couch watching a DVD with you? If you're not certain about their relaxation preference, don't guess, ask! (And make a note for a future occasion.)

Tip #9: Theater, opera, or show
Look out for something at the theater, opera,

or a show that interests your partner and try to book it in advance. It all depends on your partner's taste. Only pick the types of shows she'll enjoy.

Tip #10: Go for a walk

If that's part of what you both like, plan a walk somewhere nice or new with your partner. You can go to a nice lookout and take a bottle of wine, cheese, and crackers with you.

DATE NIGHTS AT HOME

For a lot of couples, especially those that have been together a long time, a date night is a vital way to keep their relationship fresh. While many dating advice will recommend going out to new and exciting places, at-home date night can be very rewarding as well especially with your bedroom in such close proximity for an erotic ending to the evening. The evening needs to be put together with thought and care while considering little details that will catch her attention and blow her away.

Considering her wants and tastes first when planning the evening is highly important. What kinds of food does she like? What can you cook from scratch? What manner of entertainment catches her attention? What type of decorations or room setting will please her? Candles or no candles? Any partner is pleased when a man shows a genuine awareness of what she likes.

Once you have considered your partner's likes, you need to figure out what you can do to kick it up a notch. She may say that ordering in a pizza is a good idea, but perhaps she'd be even more pleased if you could make one from scratch (assuming you're decent in the kitchen). If she says that watching a movie would be nice, don't just pick out whatever is available from the On-Demand function, instead, search for that special Romantic Comedy flick she loves or that movie she saw when she was still a little girl and has been craving to see again. Investing in a lovely bouquet of flowers for the dinner table is always a great idea; women love flowers.

Consider playing some board games, a jigsaw puzzle, or some cards. Even better, take an existing board game, then tweak and personalize it. For example, if playing a game like Monopoly where one buys properties, create cards for the properties with which you both have a personal connection (the restaurant from your first date, the hotel from a recent vacation, etc.). You can move beyond games, of course. Maybe your partner would enjoy hearing some passionate and sensual love sonnets by her favorite poet read aloud to her. You can pre-select any number of rhythmic tunes that will transform your living room into a dance floor. It could also be as simple as playing a musical instrument (if you can) for her and encouraging her to sing along.

Find ways to add a little spice to the at-home date night to make it much more special. After all, one of the benefits of staying at home on a date is that you guys can behave in a more intimate manner than in public. As always, I have some dating tips you can use or use for inspiration.

Date Tip 1: Winner Takes All. No Cell Phones.

Okay fellas, it's date night and she wants to go out. Well, you have to switch it up tonight. You two have a cook-off. She can make her best chicken or meatloaf and you can make your best spaghetti or steak. Call your married or involved friends and have them judge you. Whoever wins get to make three reasonable wishes that the other must make come true with a two-week expiration date!! So, since its couple's night at your place, you can play games and such, no spades though because some people don't know how to act if they lose. I suggest scrabble. By the way, keep the cell phones off so no one can try to sneak a game of candy crush! Anyway, just enjoy the night with your lady and your friends. I'm just trying to help.

Date Tip 2: Buy Three Get Three Free

Okay fellas, it's date night and she wants to go out. Well, it's going to be a Netflix night. But first, you're going to stop at Victoria's Secret and purchase the buy three get three free deal. You can buy three things that she wants and three things you want to see her wear. Now when you get home you have to get dinner started. I'm thinking garlic roasted chicken, rice pilaf, string beans, Sister Schubert's dinner yeast rolls and Simply Lemonade Mango flavor. Don't worry; I'll post the recipe by the time you get home Oh, and since everyone is posting about it, you might as well get some Blue Bell ice cream for dessert. Anyway, choose a chick flick movie on Netflix—there's nothing wrong with that. Some chick flicks are cool. After a good meal like that you might not be able to stay up and watch the whole movie so it's going to be a "to be continued" tomorrow night starting with the Victoria's Secret items. I'm just trying to help.

Date Tip 3: Turkey or Beef?

Okay fellas, it's date night, but due to the inclement weather you aren't going anywhere. So, here's what you do. Make a nice pot of chili and use ground turkey if you don't eat beef. Light a few scented candles, give her a nice foot rub or a back rub or both. Then get your cuddle on while watching the Friday night line-up of your favorite shows. Let her lay on you until she falls asleep; she likes that. I'm just trying to help.

Date Tip 4: Deck Party Time

Okay fellas, it's date night and she wants to go out. Well, it's the holiday weekend and it's going to start tonight. Get with your married or involved friends and you go to the couple's house that has a decent sized deck. This is new to some people, but you are going to have a deck party. One of the fellas will cook on the grill and one of the ladies is going to make some light sides. It's a long weekend so you have to pace yourself. You have at least one cookout to go to this weekend. Anyway, get the music going with the older stuff first. Have an old school dance off.

Date Tip 5: Netflix and Chill

Okay fellas, it's date night, but guess what? She doesn't want to go out. Even though Monday was a holiday, the work week was still crazy for both of you. Well, it's still all good. Tonight can be a Netflix night. Go to the spot and buy a Philly cheese steak/chicken sub and fries with your favorite beverage. For the health-conscious, you can go to Subway and grab a sandwich with baked chips or Sun Chips. Cool out on the couch and enjoy each other's company.

Date Tip 6: Let Her Spoil You

Okay fellas, it's date night and she wants to go out. Well, you don't have to worry about a thing because this one is all on her. She's got it all planned out—you know how they do. She's going to take you to a spot that has some good 'ole home-style cooking. The only problem with places like that is they might have turkey wings on the menu but only serve them on Tuesday, Wednesday, and Thursday. The fried chicken is normally good, and the homemade desserts are great. You both enjoy good conversation over a great dinner.

Afterward, you think you are going somewhere else but instead, she drives home. You're a little disappointed at first, but you don't say anything (because we don't like to start anything). So, you just chill and she goes to the room and comes back with a fresh gym bag, not any gym bag, but your favorite football team's bag. You're kind of geeked-up, but then you open it and there's a t-shirt, a hand towel, and a water bottle. Now you're not upset anymore. Oh, but she's not done, she tells you to come to the bedroom and lay down. She tells you it's time for your massage and you start singing "Happy" by Pharrell Williams, well maybe not. Anyway, she gives you a good massage session that just about puts you to sleep (but you didn't really go to sleep just yet). I'm just trying to help!

Date Tip 7: Cookbook Superpower

Okay fellas, it's date night and she wants to go out. You have a different treat in mind tonight. Instead of going out, you're going to hang in. Get the cookbook out and find a recipe that any or both of you wanted to try out. You can make a homemade pizza or turkey sausage lasagna or something nice like that. Then go to the store and purchase what you need. Choose a move on Netflix, preferably an action movie if you did the chick flick last time. Anyway, prepare the dish as the directions state; I know one of you will try to add your own twist. You can do that the next time you make it.

Date Tip 8: Life is Short, Lick the Bowl

Okay fellas, it's date night and she wants to go out. Well, you might have been in the streets for the last few weeks so it's a good night to have a night in. On your way home, stop by the store and get some groceries that you need to prepare your specialty meal. You can go with lemon pepper chicken, rice pilaf, Tuscan seasoned broccoli, and rolls (they don't have to be homemade). For dessert, you can get some Red Velvet Cake Blue Bell Ice Cream. Also, get her favorite wine if she has a favorite. Remind her of your culinary skills and how "lucky" she is to have you. After dinner, take it to the couch, watch a movie on Netflix, and finish the night off. Give her a good foot and back rub and she'll be nice and relaxed. Let her lay her head on you and watch the movie...and there you have it. I'm just trying to help!

Date Tip 9: Eat it or Starve

Okay fellas, it's date night and she really doesn't want to go out but she's in the mood for something. Well, if she didn't do much cooking for Thanksgiving, convince her to make that dish she has wanted to cook but too scared to try. Tell her how much you would appreciate it and it will be practice for her and you'll do your dish next week. If she can cook, then you're good, but if she is "culinarily challenged" (made up term), then you might be lying about how it tastes. Since you've been hitting the gym, you can make that brownie sundae with the chocolate syrup for dessert. Sit back and relax on the chill spot on the couch and enjoy the rest of your evening. I'm just trying to help!

Date Tip 10: Let it Shine

Okay fellas, it's date night and she wants to go out. Well, you are behind the eight ball with Christmas shopping and decorating the house. So, step out early to Applebee's where you can always find some type of two entrees for $20.00 deal. Then go do some quick Christmas shopping and get the tree since you decided on a real one this year. When you get home, put on that Boyz II Men Christmas CD or the Motown one. Help her decorate the tree and the rest of the house. Of course, the outside is all yours tomorrow morning. She's definitely going to appreciate this. Spend the rest of the evening decorating, signing cards, wrapping gifts, etc. It's Christmas time and I'm just trying to help!

Date Tip 11: Romantic Candlelight Dinner

Okay fellas, it's date night and she wants to do something. Well, you haven't had a quiet night at home in a while so it's about that time. Prepare her a home-cooked meal using a recipe from all the ones that have been shared on Facebook. My suggestion is the Pepperoni Casserole; it looked really good in the picture. After the candlelight dinner, get out her favorite ice cream from the freezer and share a bowl with her. I know...that's romantic. Then give her a nice shoulder and back massage. If you do it right, you just might get right. I'm just trying to help!

DINNER DATE NIGHT TIPS

Most dating relationships start with a dinner and knowing how to set the dinner up could help your odds at a second date. If you are already in a relationship, you must not cease to impress your woman by taking her out to dinners; it shows her that you still value her as much as when you first met. Knowing the person you are taking to dinner well will play a crucial role in picking where to go. Is she a vegetarian or allergic to certain foods or environments? Does she prefer dark lighting or brighter? Does she dislike crowds?

The next most important question for a dinner date is where you are going. Don't make a rookie mistake; ensure that you have been to the restaurant before. This will eradicate any potential problems that can arise. You will also know if you can afford it, whether you need a reservation or not, and how to best get there. You will also be able to inform your date of what kind of clothing will be suitable beforehand. Another interesting thing about going to the restaurant earlier is that you can scope out and target the best seats in advance. You get to ask the host or hostess if you can reserve a specific table in your desired area. Trust me, restaurants are used to people who are dating making those kinds of requests, and they don't mind.

A possibly disconcerting moment for a dinner date is being late and we can't have that. Be on time to greet your date as she arrives. If you drove there separately, ensure you have gone over how to get there together so no one (her) gets lost. Also, make sure that you have clearly communicated the time and meeting place. We don't want her wandering around wondering if she's been stood up. Having all these fine details worked out beforehand can put you at ease.

Lastly, don't forget your manners; be your finest self during your date. Even the nicest restaurant cannot save you from the repulsiveness that comes from chewing with your mouth open. Never talk with your mouth full, and when you laugh, put your hand in front of your mouth if there's food in it. Use your napkin wisely to keep your face and your clothes clean. Hell, you might not get a good night hug if your date is worried about getting food on their outfit. Even if you have been dating for a while, adhere strictly to these gentleman's rules and make sure to have a good time as well. Don't know what to do when she wants to go out to dinner? Then pick one of these dinner date tips and blow her away.

Date Tip 12: Spoil Her Rotten

Okay, fellas, it's date night. She had a rough week at work, so you have a hot bath waiting for her as soon as she gets in. She's in the tub and you wash her back. Tonight, she needs to really be pampered. Take her to her favorite restaurant, let her order an appetizer before the meal, and even a dessert afterward...and you don't even have to share. Tell her that although there isn't much you can do to make it easier at work, you can make it easier for her at home while you give her a card that says, "I got you baby!" Give her a gift certificate for a massage and facial and a little change to get lunch. She doesn't know the cleaning service will be at the house while she's gone to tighten up the spot. After she reads the card, all she can do is think to herself "that's my boo-boo right there". After dinner, you go for a drive, maybe to the beach depending where you live. Go somewhere and park in a safe place, of course, and take it back to high school. Not ALL the way back but just warm it up a little bit. On the way home just tell her how much you appreciate her. I'm just trying to help!

Date Tip 13: Walk Off that Pasta

Okay fellas, it's date night and she wants to go out. I got the perfect low-cost situation for you. Take her to Olive Garden and get the Never-Ending Pasta Bowl for $9.99; you can't beat that. You can start off with your choice of unlimited breadsticks, homemade soup, or garden-fresh salad. You also get a choice of one of 6 sauces and one of seven kinds of pasta. Now that's some good eating. You can even spring for some wine. You know, get her a little tipsy so she'll start talking a little trash to you about what's going to jump off later. After dinner, take her to the local restaurant/lounge where the older folks (cat daddies and cougars) hang out. You can line dance and work that pasta off. After you've danced and had a good time, take it to the house and keep the party going. I'm just trying to help.

Date Tip 14: Lobsters Fall in Love and Mate for Life

Okay fellas, it's date night and she wants to go out. Well take her to Red Lobster and get that Crab Fest special where you can enjoy the most succulent crab entrees like Snow Crab and Crab Butter Shrimp or Crab and Roasted Garlic Seafood Bake for under $20.00. What a deal...and don't forget you can always count on the free Cheddar Bay Biscuits. Make sure you ask for another basket at the end of your meal so you can wrap them up and take them home. After dinner, take her to check out the movie she wanted to see all week. On the way home, she's going to think about how fortunate she is to have you and she's going to show you, too, once you get home. I'm just trying to help.

Date Tip 15: It's Raining Food

Okay fellas, it's date night and she wants to go out. Well, she wants dinner and a movie and that's what she's going to get. You're going to take her to a spot where you get lots of food and it won't break the bank...Cheddar's! Yes, get the chicken tender basket with fries and she can get the grilled tilapia or whatever she wants; it doesn't matter because it's cheap. As a matter of fact, go ahead and get some dessert too. You know they have a Hot Fudge Cake Sundae and Monster Cookie Sundae. After dinner, its movie time. Guess what comes out tonight? Maybe Godzilla. She may or may not be into it, but she's full so she'll be alright. After the movie, take it on to the crib and relax. I'm just trying to help!

Date Tip 16: Buon Appetito!

Okay fellas, it's date night and she wants to go out. You want to go to Hooters and get some wings, but she's not feeling it. She wants Italian and normally what she wants she gets. Go to Carrabba's so she can enjoy all the flavors of Italy from stuffed pasta to wood-fired pizza. Either get an appetizer or a dessert, but she can't have both. I suggest the Chocolate Dream." But guess what else...they have $10 off all bottles of wine. So, keep her glass full because you know what time it is when she gets nice. Take a bottle to go and when you arrive home, check something out On-Demand. Let her lean up against you and cuddle. I know you don't like it, but it's points on the board for that. After the movie, she's still nice and tipsy off that wine, so you know what that means. I'm just trying to help.

Date Tip 17: Try Out the New Place

Okay fellas, it's date night and she wants to go out. It's a little too cool for my original suggestion, so we have to make a quick switch up. Take her to one of the new restaurants in the area. You didn't hang out last week so no need to share an appetizer. As a matter of fact, order some wine too. Just have a good time conversing with each other and enjoy the night. Then enjoy some more "conversation" later tonight. I'm just trying to help.

Date Tip 18: How About Some Poetry for Dessert

Okay fellas, it's date night and she wants to go out. Well, the weather is nice, so take her to a restaurant that has an outside dining area. Hopefully, you can find a spot with a little music playing or a live band. That would be dope. You're feeling a little romantic, so you order wine with dinner. Make sure you converse with her during the meal, be silly and playful, look into her eyes, and smile at her from time to time. They like that stuff. Make sure she gets whatever dessert she wants and tell her she deserves it. After a long dinner, you take her back home to finish the night. After she gets comfortable, you surprise her with a poem that you've been working on since Monday. Forget about watching TV because after that poem, it's on. I'm just trying to help.

Date Tip 19: Let's Wing it

Okay fellas, it's date night and she wants to go out. You don't have to be romantic all the time so go simple tonight and hit up your favorite wing spot. Hooter's, Buffalo Wild Wings, Wing Zone, Wing Bistro, Wings & Things, or whatever's your pleasure. You might have to be like Rick Ross and get some lemon pepper wings. You and your lady can sit back, cut loose, and talk trash. There's nothing like being able to laugh and joke with your boo. Anyway, after you have dined sufficiently take her to see that movie with that guy in it that all the women go crazy over...oh yeah Idris Elba in *No Good Deed* but guess what...Taraji P. Henson is in that movie, too, so you're both winning. After the movie, just call it a night and take it on to the crib. I'm just trying to help!

Date Tip 20: Get Up. Dress Up. Show Up.

Okay fellas, it's date night and she wants to go out. Well, go on an old school date where couples actually dressed up to go out. I'm not saying three-piece suit or anything but some slacks and a button down and she can wear a nice dress. If the weather is starting to get cooler, this might be the last chance for her to wear one of those outfits that shows the side boob and/or thigh meat. Both of you are looking good and smelling good. Step outside of the box and take her to get some exotic cuisine, maybe some Ethiopian or Mediterranean food. Just make sure you ask questions about the menu items because you don't want to order something you can't deal with, if you know what I mean. After dinner, take her to a grown-up club or lounge or somewhere to listen to music. You two can chill and talk or hit the dance floor. I'm sure wherever you go, the DJ will play some line dance songs. Anyway, enjoy the night. I'm just trying to help.

Date Tip 21: It Tastes Better with Family

Okay fellas, it's date night and she wants to go out. Well, it's the day after Thanksgiving and there's still plenty food at your house, your mama's house, and anybody else's house you can think of so there's no need to go out to eat. You guys probably still have enough family in town to make it a family thing. Either go to someone's house and get some games going or go out somewhere like the bowling alley. The only thing is you have to make sure your Uncle Leroy (insert other names) doesn't drink too much before going out because you know he's going to be embarrassing. Don't get too upset over who wins or loses, it's just for fun. Finish enjoying your family time. I'm just trying to help!

Date Tip 22: New Year, New Me

Okay fellas, it's date night and she wants to go out. Well, it might be the first date night in the year, so you have to start it off right. Tell her to get dressed and pack a bag. You made a reservation at a hotel, preferably Embassy Suites. After you check in, go to the free reception where you get complimentary snacks and drinks. When that's over, take her to a nice restaurant but nothing too fancy. You don't have to order appetizers because you already got straight at the hotel. You can talk about last year, what's going to be different this year...you know, the new year new me stuff. After dinner, head on back to the hotel and kick it some more at the bar, only for a little while though. Then go up to the room to unwind. You pull out your bag of tricks with some scented candles and massage oil in it. Get the mood right with the candles and give her a good back massage. After that, she's on cloud nine so let her cuddle on you for a bit and then...! When you wake up, go down and get the good complimentary breakfast. The omelets are banging so that's what I suggest. After breakfast, take her to the spa so she can get a facial and maybe a pedicure. After that, it's check out time. What a way to start out the year. I'm just trying to help!

Date Tip 23: Italian Cuisine

Okay fellas, it's date night and she's feeling international. Take her to get some Italian cuisine from Olive Garden. Start out with unlimited freshly baked breadsticks and choice of garden salad or soup. Move on to the 2 for $25 dinner and share an appetizer or dessert. There's even the Lighter Fair Menu, if you prefer, with food low in calories and big on taste all under 575 calories. Have a good night. I'm just trying to help.

Date Tip 24: Endless Appetizers!

Okay fellas, it's date night and she wants to go out. Well, tonight is simple, TGI Fridays... yes, endless appetizers for $10. Loaded Potato Skins, Pan-Seared Pot Stickers, Mozzarella Sticks, Garlic & Basil Bruschetta, Tuscan Spinach Dip, Boneless Buffalo Wings, and Crispy Green Bean Fries. There is only one kicker, you can only order one per person and that one is unlimited. If you don't want to order an entree, you really don't need to. Afterward, take her to the beach or town center area if there's a fountain and walk around for a while, enjoying the scenery. Hold her had while you're walking to show her some affection. They like that. Finish off the night on the couch with Netflix. I'm just trying to help.

UNIQUE LOCATION DATE NIGHT TIPS

There are a number of reasons the place you choose for your date is vital. First, you don't want to take your date to a place they are totally uninterested in. You must both choose a place that you jointly agree on and can have a good time. If you go to a place that makes you uncomfortable, it can damage the date and we don't want that, right? This kind of error will also show that you have poor communication skills because you didn't make it clear that you didn't want to go there.

To pick the best place for a date, you must first understand what both you and your partner wants. If either you or your partner dislikes sports, it doesn't make sense to buy tickets to a sports event. If you or she hate large crowds, it doesn't make sense to attend a crowded party. It is critical that you choose a date that perfectly matches your interests and hers. Since you are already dating, you probably have similar interests; it should be easy for you to choose a mutually suitable location for your date.

An art gallery would make a great date night for those who are intellectual or have artistic interests. Another good place for couples is a nice park or garden or a nice vacation spot. You can stroll or sit and talk about each other and various topics while enjoying each other's company. A classic option for intellectuals is the museum; it is a quiet place where you can talk about the various exhibitions in the way only intellectuals can. If you guys enjoy being in large crowds, you may want to consider going to concerts, sporting events, or even clubs. If you like to go shopping, you can spend the night going to various stores, window shopping, or otherwise. You can pick from these ideas for your next location-oriented date nights.

Date Tip 25: Commandeer a Vacation Spot

Okay fellas, it's date night and she wants to go out. She doesn't know this, but you planned a weekend getaway. Your rich engineer pal let you use his vacation spot on the beach for the weekend. So, tell her to pack a backpack and roll out. If the weather is nice enough, take a stroll on the boardwalk. Hold hands or put your arm around her...you know PDA (Public Display of Affection). She likes that stuff. Stop at a nice restaurant and grab something to eat, continuing the good conversation. Go ahead and get some good dessert too. Anyway, go back to the room and get in the Jacuzzi tub if they have one and just relax.

Date Tip 26: Jazz it up a Little

Okay fellas, it's date night and she wants to go out. Well, it's Halloween and she is feeling a little jazzy. There is a Halloween/Costume Party or Masquerade Ball you have tickets to. She picked out her costume weeks ago, and it's showing off her figure that has improved since she has been working hard in the gym. You have your costume as well, and it compliments hers. Now, when you arrive at the party, don't spend the whole night joking at what other people are wearing. Especially those folks who have on costumes they have absolutely no business wearing....but then again that's kind of fun. Anyway, make sure you get her on the dance floor and let her get her Beyoncé on. You can even start the proverbial "soul train" line. So, just enjoy the night out in your costumes. When you get home, let her know you want your other treat. I'm just trying to help!

Date Tip 27: Paint your Heart

Okay fellas, it's date night and she wants to go out. Well, have a date night with a twist or some paint. Basically, you will go to a specific location and an art instructor will assist you in creating your own painting in acrylic or watercolor. This could be a fun double date as well. While this is going on you, can sip on your favorite beverage. You alcoholics will have to be careful not to get wasted because your painting might turn out crazy, but then again maybe it'll be something special. Although you'll have aprons on, make sure you wear something you don't mind getting messy just in case of an accident. You can joke on each other's art or garbage; it's a matter of interpretation. When you get home, let her decide where the paintings will be placed. This will be a night to remember. I'm just trying to help!

Date Tip 28: The Legendary Cheesecake Factory

Okay fellas, it's date night and she definitely wants to go out since you hung out with the boys last week. Since you're playing make up, don't go for the specials. Go ahead and take her someplace nice. I don't mean Ruth's Chris nice though. Maybe Cheesecake Factory or something like that. And don't even share dessert. Let her order whatever kind of cheesecake she wants and one to take home too. Now you're earning points and are right back in the game. I'm just trying to help!

Date Tip 29: Shop Til' You Drop

Okay fellas, it's date night and she wants to go out. Well, tis' the season to be jolly and all that good stuff. So, start out by going shopping. She will appreciate it. Use this time to help her pick out those small gifts for your close co-workers or friends she normally exchanges gifts with. After that, you can use your Groupon deal to go somewhere and eat. Remember, you're still saving money for Christmas shopping. After dinner, go back to the crib, grab the wine, and help wrap the gifts. You'll really get some extra points for that. I'm just trying to help.

Date Tip 30: Laughter is the Best Medicine

Okay fellas, it's date night and she wants to go out. This is another simple one. Go to Carrabba's web site and sign up to get 15% off of your entire meal. All you have to do is enter your email address. So that means you can splurge a little bit and get separate desserts LOL. Oh, and it doesn't include alcohol, so plan accordingly. Anyway, relax and wind down over some delightful Italian cuisine. If you had a week like I had, then you need some laughter in your life. Take her to the local comedy club for some good laughs. You might have to drive 15 to 30 minutes to the next city but that's okay. Both of you just need to take a load off. Enjoy the atmosphere and the comedy and continue to have a good time. After the show, you make your way to the crib. During the drive home, take her by the hand and just let her know how special she is and how much she means to you. You might want to practice because you don't do this often and some of you aren't good communicators. But seriously, sometimes your lady just needs to be reminded of where she stands with you and that will take you a long way. I'm just trying to help!

Date Tip 31: Take More Chances, Dance More Dances

Okay fellas, it's date night and she wants to go out. When you walk in the house, start singing Johnny Gill's "My My My." Just tell her to put on those dark blue jeans with them long leather boots (my favorite get up). Take her to a nice soul food restaurant or something close to it. Have a nice meal along with some good conversation. Now you know women like a man who can communicate. After dinner head on over to a nice club/lounge (that might be the dinner spot). Preferably a "grown folks" joint so you don't have to deal with any foolishness. Make sure you dance with her too. Don't hug the wall while she two steps by herself and then get mad when the old Himalaya Playa grabs her by the hand and tries to rock with her. Enjoy yourselves dancing the night away and laughing at some of the outfits other people have on. I'm just trying to help!

Date Tip 32: Operation Get Fit

Okay fellas, it's date night and she wants to go out. You have something special in store for her tonight. You go pull out all that new gym gear she bought you at the beginning of the year. Well, tonight is the night. That's right, take her on a date to the gym. There are plenty of gyms and fitness centers that stay open late and the sales reps are there late too. So, go ahead, get your water bottles and towels and roll out. Start her out on the elliptical bike for cardio. Then hit the weights for biceps and triceps. You can't do too much because it's the first day at it. After the workout, hit the smoothie spot or you can stop by the store and get the ingredients to make your own. This is the beginning of "Operation Get Fit" or whatever you want to call it. Later on at the crib, she's going to complain of soreness. That's when you put those magic hands to work and give her a good massage. She'll be done after that. I'm just trying to help.

Date Tip 33: TGI...The First Friday of the Month

Okay fellas, it's date night and she wants to go out. It's an easy one tonight. If it is the first Friday of the month then I'm sure somebody somewhere is having some type of First Friday's event at an establishment in your area. Swing by there and kick it with folks you may or may not know. It's all in having a good time and you never know what connections you might make. If you're not too tired afterward maybe hit up a movie or something. I'm just trying to help.

Date Tip 34: The Celebration of Lights

Okay fellas, it's date night and she wants to go out. Well, you spent all your money trying to satisfy everyone for Christmas. But, she STILL wants to go out. Don't fret; you got that free pass from the job to see "The Celebration of Lights" or whatever it's called in your city. Oh, and your auntie blessed you with that $25.00 movie theater gift card. Now go back home and finish off that lemon pound cake or that red velvet cake from Christmas dinner and just chill. So, there you have it—the cheapest date of the year. I'm just trying to help!

Date Tip 35: Annual Holiday Parties

Okay fellas, it's date night and she wants to go out. Your job is having its Annual Holiday Party at the local restaurant/lounge so just take her there. Make sure she wears those heals that make it jump! You know what I mean. Anyway, eat, drink, socialize, and introduce her to everyone at the job who hasn't met her yet. Just remember not to flirt with the receptionist whom you have borderline inappropriate dialogue with on occasion. That woman's intuition will kick your butt and you will be on the couch tonight. After a couple of hours, just take it on to crib because you are going out again tomorrow night. I'm just trying to help.

Date Tip 36: Family Getaway

Okay fellas, it's date night and she wants to go out. Since family is still in town for the weekend, everyone should go out and do something fun. So, heat up some leftovers, have dinner, and go bowling. Make it a competition and talk plenty of trash. Post on social media about how terrible so and so is at bowling. You can't stay out too late because the more seasoned folks have to get to bed and wake up at the crack of dawn.. Anyway, there's nothing like family time, right? I'm just trying to help!

Date Tip 37: The Reward for Good Behavior

Okay fellas, it's date night and she wants to go out. Go to your nearest shopping area and do some pre-Christmas browsing to see what you're going to get your family/friends. This will also give you the opportunity to let her know what she could get if she acts right. Then go to a spot like Buffalo Wild Wings or Hooters and get your eat and drink on. Now after that, go to the movies. I'm just trying to help.

Date Tip 38: Eat While You Still Have Teeth

Okay fellas, it's date night. But guess what? It's a little cold and she really doesn't want to go out. She said she is the mood to chill and eat some pizza. Fix her a nice hot bath with that aromatherapy stuff. Make sure you wash her back and comb her hair even. She might have gotten the short natural on you by now so you may have to brush it. Then hit up your nearest spot, no not Domino's or Pizza Hut. You have to go to Ricco's, Andrea's, Marco's, Anna's or something with a name like that to get that good, authentic tasting pizza. Those spots don't have specials either. Stop by the store and get some dessert, ice cream, cake, or cookies. Go back to the crib, watch a good movie, and enjoy the rest of the night. I'm just trying to help.

Date Tip 39: Let God In

Okay fellas, it's date night and she wants to go out. Well, it's time for some spiritual growth and development, according to her anyway. Your lady's co-worker has a sister whose friend's church's Couples Ministry is having a program tonight. I know you don't want to go but trust me; you will earn major points for this one. Besides, they're going to discuss some of the issues you have with her too. Don't say too much or you'll end up in the doghouse and sleeping on the couch and not getting any action. Afterward, take her to Outback and get the Steak and Unlimited Shrimp for $14.99. You can get her a dessert too. You can discuss some of the things she learned over dinner. Now when you get to the crib, just grab her up, take her to the bedroom and...BOOM! I'm just trying to help!

Date Tip 40: I'd Rather Be Fishing

Okay fellas, it's date night and she wants to go out. Well, if there's nothing really going on in the city then you can do something recreational. You're a nature boy at heart so take her night fishing on a 24-hour fishing pier. Make sure to pack a lunch because buying food from the pier is almost like going to the concession stand at the movies. Make sure to pack the hand sanitizer and some paper towels. You can bring the iPod with the speakers too; party on the pier. By the way, she has to bait her own hook and take the fish off too; you can do that for her if she needs you to. Just have fun on the water whether you leave with a cooler full of fish or an empty cooler. But if all goes well, fish fry tomorrow at the crib. I'm just trying to help!

Date Tip 41: Roller Coaster of Love

Okay fellas, it's date night and she wants to go out. Just start singing...5...5...5-dollar foot long, from Subway. Yes, that's about it, because you are not going out tonight, you have to get some rest. Tomorrow is amusement park day (Busch Gardens, Kings Dominion, Six Flags or whatever park that's close to you. You can save some money and pack your lunch so you don't have to buy that expensive stuff inside the park. Maybe a funnel cake but nothing else.. Anyway, don't let her punk out on the roller coasters either. Front car, front seat, hands up the whole way. That's how you do it. Make sure she wears her comfortable shoes, too, because you know she'll stop and want to sit on the bench too many times. As a bonus, pack a bag and stay overnight and do the roller coaster back in the room. I'm just trying to help.

Date Tip 42: Let Loose

Okay fellas, it's date night and she wants to go out. She feels like dancing because she hasn't cut a rug in quite some time, and she's ready to let loose. No clubs,, though so check out the nearest Que, Kappa, Delta, AKA, Mason or Motorcycle Club member, etc. One of these groups is probably having a party tonight for their scholarship fund or whatever benevolent activity they're trying to support. The only thing is it might be a BYOB joint so you might just have to stop at the "licka sto" and get your goodies. Remember the theme "Party with a Purpose" and do your thing. I'm just trying to help.

Date Tip 43: Eat, Shop, Relax

Okay fellas, it's date night and she wants to go out, but the weather is messing things up and she does not want to ruin her hairdo. So, tell her to save her new outfit for next week. Since you're not going out, go to Church's Chicken and get the 8-piece dark with the large fried okra. Hit the grocery store and get some Simply Lemonade with Mango. Let her choose a chick flick to watch for the night. *Pretty Woman* is my all-time favorite, so you can't go wrong with that. After a meal like that, you won't be up too long.

Date Tip 44: Nothing Beats Live Music

Okay fellas, it's date night and she wants to go out. It's a little warm outside so when it cools a bit, take her to your downtown or city center area for the block party or free outside live entertainment. Walk around and enjoy the music and the scenery. Showing a little PDA might go a long way later tonight. Hold her hand a few times, or while you're walking, place your hand on the lower part of her back. On the way home, stop at the grocery store (it might have to be Wal-Mart if it's too late) and get her favorite ice cream. After you get settled in, fix her a bowl. and enjoy the rest of the night watching TV. I'm just trying to help!

Date Tip 45: Plenty of Fish

Okay fellas, it's date night and she wants to go out. Well, if it's summer, do something you haven't done all summer long. Take her fishing. Pick one of those all-night fishing piers. But first, you have to get some snacks and drinks and don't forget the hand sanitizer either.

Also, pack your bag chairs as well because standing up all night isn't the play. Now, if you can swing by a bait shop or a seafood market that sells bait then you're better off getting it from there because buying bait at the pier is like buying food from the movie theater. The prices are inflated. She's been fishing before, so she knows what to do. Yes, she can put the bait on the hook and take the fish off the hook as well. Enjoy the night air while fishing and spending some quality time together. Hopefully, you'll catch a cooler full so you can have a mini fish fry at the crib tomorrow afternoon or have some for the tailgate.

MOVIE NIGHT DATE TIPS

Dinner and a movie has been the standard and favored first date since your parents and your grandparents went out on dates. Catching a flick at a theater is a really great way to chill out, spend quality time with friends and partners, all while enjoying the fun and unique stories being told on the screen. Nowadays, there are so many movies coming out and the time from theatrical release to DVD release is getting considerably shorter so much that it can be hard to keep up with what you or your partner want. When you are picking a movie for a date, whether a first date or your girlfriend, the decision is even more crucial. Here are seven ways to choose perfect date night movies.

1. Find out some previous movies your date liked
While having regular conversations, try to pay attention to what kind of things your date enjoys. This could give you important clues as to the sort of movies they might enjoy. When you are talking about flicks you've seen, note what they say are there favorites and dislikes and try to choose new releases accordingly. Listening is the perfect way to know what a good choice is based on what she has enjoyed in the past.

2. Find similar movies

If you already have a short list of her preferred movies, go online and find out some similar movies. You can pick the ones directed by the same person, movies that have similar main casts, similar premises, or movies that are simply in the same genre. Today, superhero movies tend to have keywords like "universe" or imaginary worlds at the center of different films and diverse storylines.

3. Try a movie that merges different genres together

As a compromise, if your taste differs from your date's, you might be able to compromise conveniently by choosing a movie that effectively blends both genres together. For example, if she enjoys horror, and you prefer comedy, a dark comedy might do the trick. Rom-com vs action? There are numerous movies that are full of action but still successfully blend romance and humor as well. There is always something for everyone when you compromise in this manner.

4. Pick a sequel or prequel

A worthy sequel or a good prequel is a great way to see a newly released movie that you know your date will love. Prequels are gradually becoming more popular and they allow for more storyline to be effectively infused into the canon of the original films without having to change the ending.

5. Try watching something outside your preferences

If you or your date are feeling like it, try selecting a movie at random or intentionally selecting a movie you both think you might not be interested in. It's a good way to add a little bit of adventure into your joint decision. Who knows, you might be on your way to watching your new favorite movie!

6. Check local listings and online reviews

An easy way to select a suitable movie to watch is to check local listings and local movie review sites either in print or online sites. You'll get to see reviews and a quick synopsis of the film so you can make an informed decision.

Your date night has to be fun and a movie can make it so if you select the right one. On its own, however, a movie alone can prove to be insufficient. This is so because you might not get to talk or discuss throughout the movie so you might compensate for that with dinner before or after the movie or a walk down the street. And if she prefers to stay at home but still want to see a movie, you can watch one from the comfort of your living room on Netflix. Below are some movie tips you can use to spice up your date nights:

Date Tip 46: Cinebistro and Chill

Okay fellas, it's date night and she wants to go out. Call her on the way home from work and tell her to put on her red silk dress and her high heels. Stop by Charming Charlie's and get her a few things before going home, but keep the gift items in the car. When you go out, she will see the bag on the front seat and instantly melt. Anyway, roll on out to Cinebistro and enjoy a nice dinner and a movie. You have to touch her hand and her knee a few times throughout the movie though. And if you're feeling really froggy, go ahead and touch her thigh too. After the movie you can stroll over to the bar or lounge area and have a few drinks, laugh, and joke and reminisce about when she first tried to holler at you and the first date too. After that, take it on home because you are going to the Ques All White Party tomorrow night! I'm just trying to help.

Date Tip 47: Press Play and Wait for the Rain

Okay fellas, it's date night but she does not want to go out. It's supposed to rain later, and she can't mess that hair up. She hasn't gone to the natural yet so getting her hair wet is not cool. But since you are getting up early in the morning anyway for a couple's pampering; manicure, pedicure, facial care, etc., just stay in the crib and make it a Netflix night. You pick a movie, she also gets to pick a movie and you decide whose pick was the best after you watch them both. Besides, you're saving money on dinner and an extra trip to the hair salon. I'm just trying to help.

Date Tip 48: Up next, Romantic Drama

Okay fellas, it's date night and she wants to go out. Well, it's cold and she got some gears in the closet she's been waiting to wear. Tell her to put on your favorite outfit—nice fitted jeans and some high boots. Take her to an early dinner to Outback or Texas Roadhouse or something like that. After dinner, take her to see the newly-released romantic drama. Anyway, after the movie take it to the crib especially if it's cold that night. Once you get home and get comfortable, fix some hot chocolate and mellow out on the couch for the rest of the night. I'm just trying to help.

Date Tip 49: Reminisce with a Smile

Okay fellas, it's date night. This one is simple. Take her to the movies and then go for dessert, coffee, or a cappuccino afterward for some good conversation. You can play "remember when" and reflect on the good times. You have to keep your charm and sense of humor on point. BUT don't forget to listen. I'm just trying to help.

Date Tip 50: Watch Then Review

Okay fellas, it's date night and she wants to go out. Well, last week you might have felt you went all out so tonight is going to be a little simple. You can't have her thinking that was going to be an-every-week thing. Anyway, check out Groupon for some restaurants in your local area. They really have some good deals and I'm pretty sure you can find something to go with. After dinner, you go to the movies. After the movie, take it to the crib. You can discuss the movie. By the way, get the hot cocoa ready before you settle down. If she gets cold, let her snuggle with you. You know how they do. I'm just trying to help.

Date Tip 51: Fifty Shades

Okay fellas, it's date night and she wants to go out. The snow is melting and it's not that cold so roll with it. Do something really simple. Hit up Applebee's for the 2 for $20 Showdown.

It's oayk to be frugal sometimes. You can choose two of seven entrees and one of five appetizers. You can add another appetizer or just share. And you could even get dessert too. My suggestion is that Blue Ribbon Brownie or the Triple Chocolate Meltdown. After your delicious, flavorful meal, go ahead and take her to the movies. Yeah, you didn't take her to see 50 Shades of Grey when it came out for Valentine's Day and the word is it's not as good as it was thought to be, but you bite the bullet and go anyway. Little sacrifices bro...it's okay. After the movie, take it on to the crib and show her 50 shades of you. I'm just trying to help!

Date Tip 52: Let the Tears Flow

Okay fellas, it's date night and she wants to go out. Today is Friday, so take her to TGI Fridays. You can get the 2 for $10 special. That's right, an appetizer and entree for $10. That deal is so good she can get her own dessert. After dinner, go check out *12 Years a Slave*. Make sure you have some tissue for her because she might cry. Anyway, you can discuss the movie on the way home. When you get home, fix her some hot cocoa so she can warm up a tad bit. Settle on the couch and watch TV while you and the hot cocoa are warming her up. I'm just trying to help!

Date Tip 53: Wing It at The Movies

Okay fellas, it's date night and she wants to go out. You haven't been to a good movie in a while and neither has she. Well, *The Butler* is still out, and you can go and get some education and entertainment. Since movie concession food is so expensive, just stop by the chicken spot on your way and get some wings. You should have told her to take the big no named bag and not the Michael Kors. You know it will be a cold day in hell before any food is going in the MK bag no matter how tight the chicken is wrapped. Now the movie has been out for a while so there should be plenty of seats so no need to be all close to anyone. You don't want them asking for a wing. Anyway, after the movie you can take her to Cold Stone because you got that $10 for $6 deal off of Groupon. She likes the way you save. I'm just trying to help.

LOW BUDGET DATE NIGHT IDEAS

Nowadays everyone is looking to save a penny or two, but that doesn't mean that your dating life has to suffer! There are plenty of creative and fun ways to treat your honey to a fun night without breaking the bank. This doesn't mean that your significant other won't appreciate a big night on the town every now and then, but the dates that cost you less can be just as exciting and enjoyable as those that cost you an arm and a leg. Low budget dating does not mean staying in every night either, there are still plenty of options to get you out of the house and into the dating scene.

While spending a small fortune at a fancy restaurant is fine on important occasions such as birthdays and anniversaries, it isn't very practical for every date. Plus, treating your partner to big lavish dates on a regular basis will take the special aspect out of it and won't give you much to look forward to. Instead of picking the swankiest restaurant in town, try checking out the local diner for some good home cooked meal and jazzy atmosphere. Or if you have already eaten, diners are a great place to drink a coffee and sample some killer desserts. If the diner isn't your style, take your date out for drinks and appetizers instead. This is a great way to cut down on expensive meals for low budget dating while still bringing your significant other to the new hotspots in town.

Another great alternative to eating out is cooking at home. Everyone enjoys a home cooked meal after a long day, so don't be afraid to exhibit your culinary genius for your date. If you aren't a big cook, stick to the dishes that you know you can pull off without burning the house down. Also, cooking together can be a fun and relaxing way to spend time with each other. Making dinner together with a bottle of wine and soft jazz music in the background is a great way to spend a quiet evening together without spending a ton of money.

A great way to spice up an ordinary home-cooked meal is to turn it into a picnic. Picnic style dates are always fun and easily arranged for low budget dating. Bring the feast outside by candlelight for a romantic night under the stars or just spread a blanket on the living room floor to avoid the bugs! During the day, go for a walk in the local park or ecological reserve and bring something to snack on. Spreading a blanket and spending time with each other outdoors is a great way to bring couples closer without spending a ton of money. For daytime picnics, bring finger foods such as fresh fruit, crackers, and cheese to munch on or add a bottle of wine for nighttime picnics. Since dining out can be an expensive date, try these alternatives to save a few pennies while still enjoying a delicious meal with your special somebody. Here are some tips you can use to show your girl a good time while saving some money; some of them are a little crafty.

Date Tip 54: Nah, Not Interested

Okay fellas, it's date night. Take your lady to that resort that's been calling and begging you to visit. Check in tonight and wake up in the morning and take the 90-minute tour. Tell them you're not interested after you get reimbursed for the two-night stay and your $50 gift certificate to the fancy restaurant up the street. What a weekend. I'm just trying to help!

Date Tip 55: Jump in on Killer Deals

Okay fellas, it's date night and she wants to go out. It's a little dreary outside, but that's okay because it's not a stay out all night date anyway. Living Social and Groupon have some killer deals this week. You can get 50% off a local restaurant. Now it might not be her favorite but since you're paying...uh LOL. Anyway, pick one of them and head out. I say make it Italian so it can seem at least somewhat romantic. Once home, watch a movie or two on Netflix and just chill for the rest of the night. I'm just trying to help.

Date Tip 56: The Birthday Trick

Okay fellas, it's date night and she wants to go out. You went a little hard last week so you can be El Cheapo tonight; I mean, be a little frugal. Take her to Red Lobster for the Seafood Dinner for Two for $25.00. Load up on the Cheddar Bay Biscuits instead of ordering an appetizer. Instead of sharing the dessert that comes after the meal, tell the server it's her birthday and get another dessert for free. Once home, pick a movie on Netflix to watch and fall asleep on. I'm just trying to help.

Date Tip 57: Dirty Talk Friday

Okay fellas, it's date night and she wants to go out. I have a smoking deal for you. T.G.I. Fridays 2 for $10 offer. You can get an appetizer and an entree for the really low price of $10. The weather has been so hot, so you need some cold dessert. Go to your local Cold Stone, Baskin Robbins or wherever they sell good ice cream and get some. Sit outside and enjoy the night air; hopefully, the humidity goes down. Now while you're chilling, talk a little trash to her. Tell her how you like the way she's eating that ice cream. Tell her how good she looks and smells, and how you're in the mood. After that take it on home and finish dessert. I'm just trying to help.

Date Tip 58: PDA for Some Results

Okay fellas, it's date night and she wants to go out. It's a little warm outside so when it cools a bit, take her to your downtown or city center area for the block party and/or free outside live entertainment. Walk around and enjoy the music and the scenery. Showing a little PDA might go a long way later tonight. Hold her hand a few times or while you're walking place your hand on the lower part of her back. On the way home, stop at the grocery store (it might have to be Wal-Mart if it's too late) and get her favorite ice cream. After you get settled in, fix her a bowl, and enjoy the rest of the night watching TV. I'm just trying to help!

Date Tip 59: Hit Up Subway

Okay fellas, it's date night and she wants to go out. Well, you just had Thanksgiving last week with leftovers going into the weekend and the Christmas holiday is right around the corner. So, you're going to want to eat light and spend light as well. Hit up Subway for a delicious healthy meal. You know they have the Simple 6 Menu, a choice of 6 of their best six-inch subs plus chips and a drink for $6.00. Or you can get the customer appreciation deal, $2.00 off of a six-inch Cold Cut Combo or a six-inch Meatball Marinara. Once home, watch a movie or two on Netflix. Spend the night in the crib and save some money for your Christmas shopping. I'm just trying to help.

Date Tip 60: Four Course Fiesta Italiana, Yummy!

Okay fellas, it's date night and she wants to go out. Well, you weren't really planning on doing anything because it's, but you got wind of the deal at Olive Garden. They have the Four Course Fiesta Italiana starting at $12.99. You can get unlimited soup or salad and breadsticks, choice of 1 of 3 appetizers, choice of 1 of 6 delicious main courses and choice of 1 of 5 desserts. You might just spring for a bottle. Enjoy your meal and the good company. Make it a short night and go back home chill at the crib. I'm just trying to help!

Date Tip 61: Time Your Budget

Okay fellas, it's date night! Guess what's back: the $20 dinner for two at Chili's! Share an appetizer and then choose two entrees like that new Parmesan-Crusted Steak or the Mango Chili-Tilapia. Then hit your local bowling alley and have some fun. Try to get there before 10 pm because some places jack up the prices for games and shoe rentals as it gets later. Don't let her win either...beat her like you would one of your boys. I'm just trying to help.

Date Tip 62: Time to Use That Coupon

Okay, fellas, it's date night. We're going to keep it simple and frugal. Print out your coupon for $10 off two entrees at Outback Steakhouse. Go ahead and share an appetizer while you're at it. Then go to the restaurant/lounge where your co-worker is celebrating their birthday— one drink limit. I'm just trying to help.

There you have it, a comprehensive yet easy to use collection of dating tips. One last tip before we go—enjoy!